Mike Peyton's cartoons are a regular feature in yachting magazines in a number of countries. Six books by him have been published in this present series, *Come Sailing* (1975), *Come Sailing Again* (1976), *Hurricane Zoe and Other Sailing* (1977), *Finish with Engines* (1979), *They Call It Sailing* (1981) and *The Pick of Peyton* (1983). The last named contained the most popular drawings from all the others which had quickly sold out. He also runs a charter business, using his 38-foot ketch, *Touchstone,* operating from Maldon, Essex. With his wife, Kathleen, author of the 'Flambards' novels, he lives at nearby Fambridge on the River Crouch.

OUT OF OUR DEPTH

Mike Peyton

NAUTICAL

Many of these cartoons first appeared in either
Yachts and Yachting or *Practical Boat Owner.*

Published in Great Britain 1985 by
NAUTICAL BOOKS
an imprint of Conway Maritime Press Ltd
24 Bride Lane, Fleet Street
London EC4Y 8DR

ISBN 0 85177 353 2

Filmset by Trevor Ridley Creative Services, Southend-on-Sea
Printed by Bath Press, Bath

Contents

Introduction

In my early sailing days doom and disaster — the
basis of many a cartoon idea — came thick and
fast, in fact, often, too quick and too fast. I could
easily get six cartoon ideas before I had cleared
the moorings. But gradually over the years as
gribble was overtaken by osmosis, my own self-
generated ideas got more scarce — months
between disasters instead of, as in the old days,
minutes or even, early on it seemed, seconds
between incidents.

Then there came a lull, a slight vacuum and,
as you know, nature abhors a vacuum. That is
why I drifted into chartering, drawn that way, I
like to think, by the same natural law as that of
the moon attracting the tides. Everyone knows
the theory behind chartering: you take people
sailing who pay you for it, and you make a profit.
That's a joke to start with.

However, charterers see everyday incidents
with a fresh, irrational and innocent eye which is
now beyond my more experienced, even
jaundiced, view. They also cause incidents to
happen with their fresh, irrational and innocent
actions, try as I can with all my experience to
prevent them. So, as grey hairs grew (prematurely I
like to think, prompted by these occupational
hazards) I used my charterers' innocent remarks
and actions to provide cartoon ideas.

And so, to them I dedicate this book.

North Fambridge, 1985   MP

7

Out of our depth

'Well, we made it.'

'According to the wind indicator it's easing.'

'Some day, skip, we'll look back on this and laugh —
won't we?'

'Notice the forecast is never wrong when it's a bad one
on the nose.'

'I know navigation is not an exact science, but I expect it
more exact than that.'

'There are occasions when my wife's opinion on sailing has some truth in it.'

'Now listen what you've got to do — strip off, tie a line
around yourself with a bowline as I've shown you,
get the bread knife . . .'

'*It's times like these that I seem to lose my sense of adventure.*'

*'I think we can relax, we must have passed that unlit buoy
by now.'*

*'Re your earlier remark: "there's the West Hinder just where
it should be . . ."'*

'With luck he'll get the tides wrong, again — and drown.'

'John, that lighthouse you said pinpointed our position
and which I had to steer for . . .'

Shore based

'What do you expect if you buy him a pair of winches for Christmas; of course he'll go and fit them.'

'What the hell do you mean — I'm lucky?'

'It's a wonderful forecast: gales in all areas . . .'

'You know Keith, it's only when I get ashore that I can truly relax.'

25

'Reg, are you ready, Reg . . . Reg . . .'

'It's a pity your office doesn't work on HW Dover . . . you
wouldn't be late so often.'

'. . . and then I remembered I hadn't drained the engine.'

'But it's stored under cover now, that's why our rates have gone up.'

*'Looks like a weekend for Brownie points, Reg, —
gardening!'*

'It's not the boat that chokes me off, it's the subsidized council
house.'

'We were thinking of getting something bigger.'

'It will be interesting to hear Sue's version of the trip.'

'All right you've nagged me into it: we'll go to your sister's wedding this afternoon.'

Working on it

'A yachtsman are you, sir? Dressed like that at two in the morning with a box of tools . . . come and tell the Sergeant.'

'Bit of a hiccup, Joe! When you took that engine out, did you
realize the fool of an owner hadn't turned the water intake
off?'

'Up a bit, and left.'

'Yes, we've got her in, but . . .'

'You're not the only one who had a big work programme
planned for this weekend.'

'When I asked you to plant a rose bush, you had a bad back.'

'They'll be telling each other how far behind they are with
their work programme.'

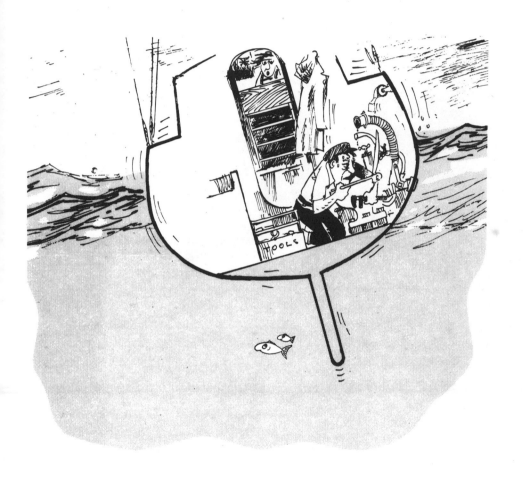

'. . . and hurry.'

'It's a bit pathetic, all that aggro over a drop of paint.'

'Ready?'

Ships that pass and sometimes meet

'Always play safe and go astern of them.'

*'I don't know if he heard you shout "starboard" but I'm
pretty sure he heard "stupid bastard".'*

'Can we try and work out logically what's happened?'

'I always need a couple of weekends after a boat show to get
back to reality.'

'Reckon he's not as fast as he thought he was Fred — cut the engine.'

'They must be bored stiff on board, if they need bars, discos,
cinemas, restaurants . . .'

'I always think there's something exciting in the phrase
"clearing harbour".'

'I told you, you need more weight on that mackerel line.'

'I do beg your pardon.'

Safe alongside

'I said "Clacton Pier".'

'Mummy's all right — just hurry up.'

'I told you to ship it.'

'You can't lie there, I'm leaving soon.'

'Of course it will be strong enou . . .'

'Hey! that's my line you're cutting.'

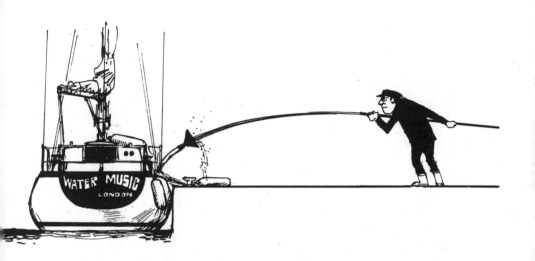

'What does he mean darling, foxtrot - oscar!'

'But I sail to get away from my wife too.'

'Hop ashore with a line, darling — quick you stupid bit . . .!!!'

'It might seem a cheap winter's berth to you but it doesn't
to me.'

Gone foreign

'Customs, had a good trip?'

'I know what that Frenchman was rabbiting on about now...'

'I don't give a damn about the forecast . . . at 80 francs a
night we sail on.'

'Je think the drapeau francais is tres jolie.'

'You must admit it was a good idea of mine to sell the house
and sail . . .'

'Act the stupid Anglais, pretend you don't know what he
wants.'

'You should have been here yesterday.'

'Of course, I'm worried, you said we would be in Calais for lunch.'

'They do say there's nothing like a small boat for getting to know people.'

Class I to V

'I find they vary considerably. Some are friendly and pleasant and others are ill-mannered and foul-mouthed.'

'Sorry Skip, my mistake, five to port.'

'I'm sorry, I misjudged that, I'd like it down.'

'I agree, a poor race and not our sort of weather either.'

'I know my rights — ready about.'

'Don't get off Joan, just pass me that sail bag.'

'I know what I'm doing — hug the sands, cheat the tide and
tack when we can lay the mark.'

' "B" means shortened course; they've finally realized there's
no wind.'

'Must have been a mark for the offshore boys.'

'And don't talk to me like that! I'm your wife not your crew.'

Confined waters

'OK George, we cleared it.'

'Hop on, John, she's away.'

'If you hadn't stowed the sails, the engine wouldn't have stopped.'

'All you have to do is to grab the mooring, take a turn and get
the headsail down, I'll do the clever stuff.'

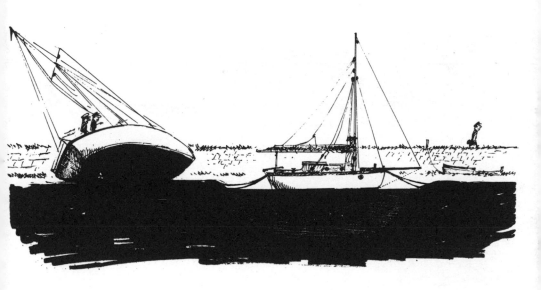

'You were right. He's a local — and he knew what he was doing.'

'I've had enough: I'm going home.'

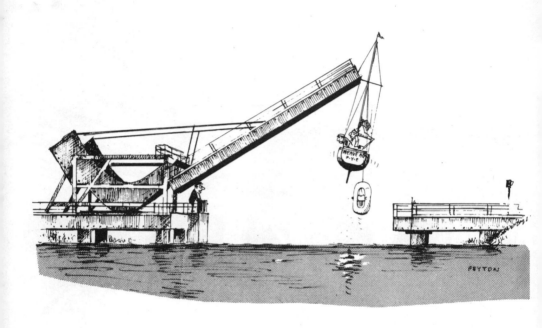

'You shouldn't be so darned impatient.'

'John, are you awake? I can hear the water coming back.'

'It's not often that one gets the chance of a nice long chat.'